DOT-TO-DOT
ON THE
SEASHORE

Karen Bryant-Mole

Illustrated By Graham Round

Edited by Jenny Tyler

On the way

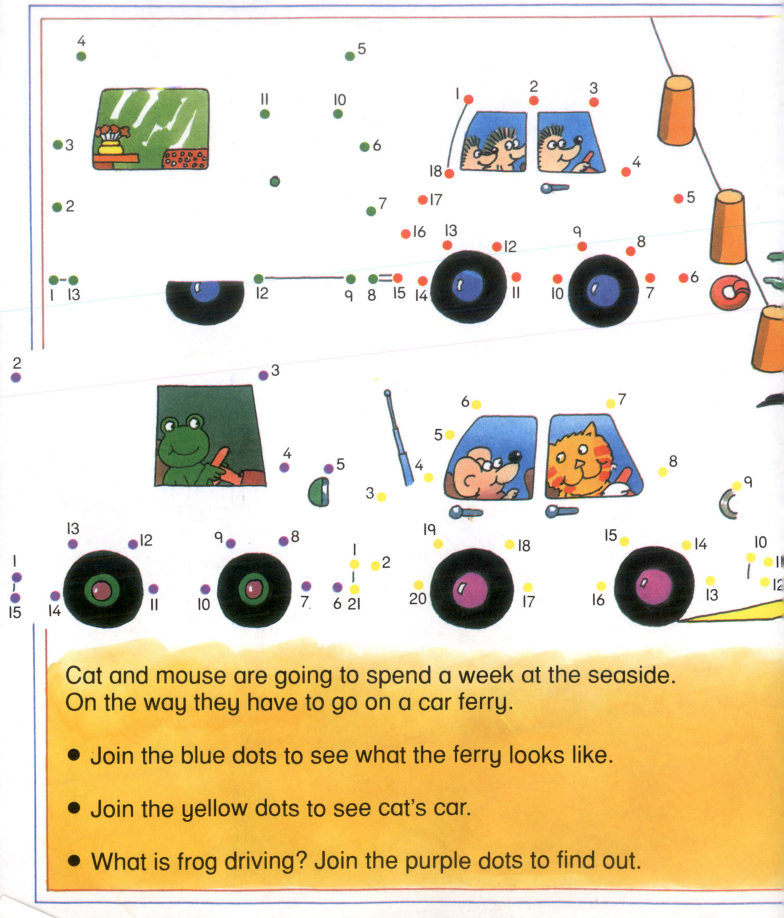

Cat and mouse are going to spend a week at the seaside.
On the way they have to go on a car ferry.

- Join the blue dots to see what the ferry looks like.

- Join the yellow dots to see cat's car.

- What is frog driving? Join the purple dots to find out.

3 4 5 6 7 8 9 10 11 12 13 14 15 16 17 18 19 20 21 22 23 24

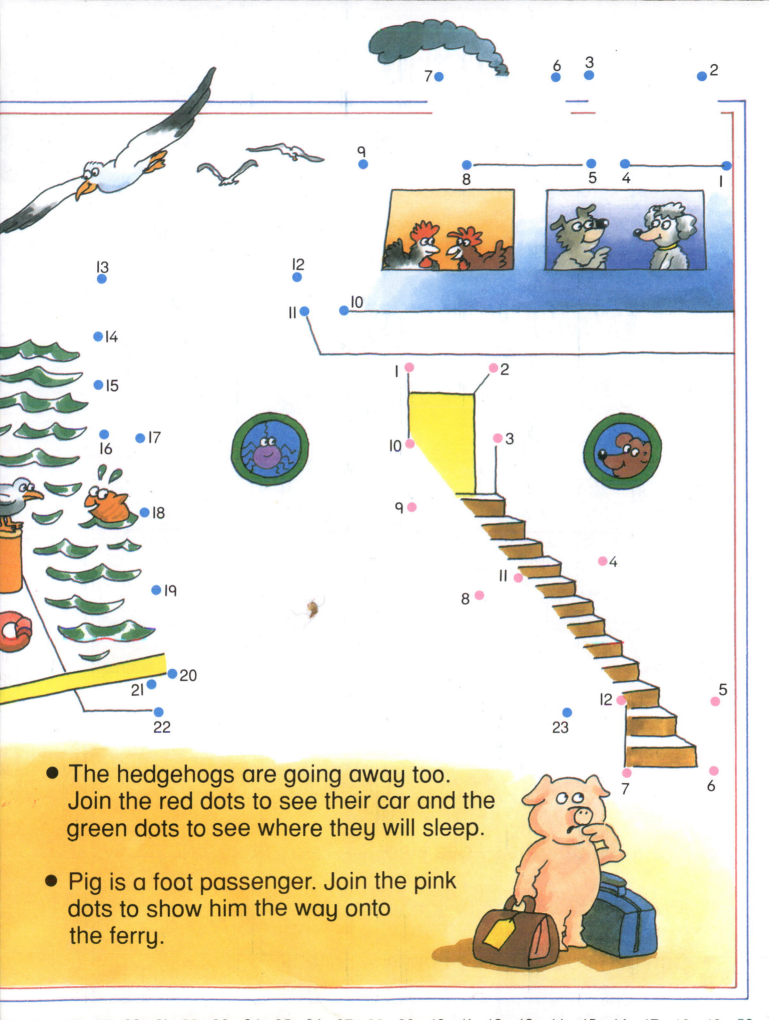

- The hedgehogs are going away too. Join the red dots to see their car and the green dots to see where they will sleep.

- Pig is a foot passenger. Join the pink dots to show him the way onto the ferry.

The house by the sea

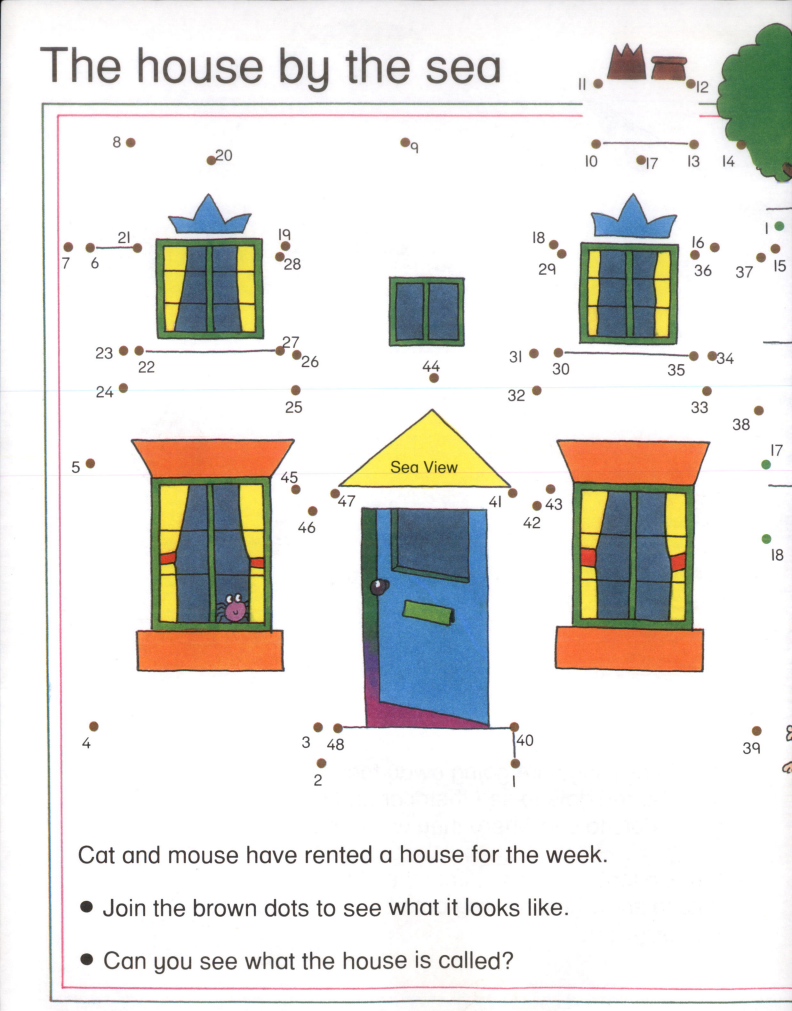

Cat and mouse have rented a house for the week.

- Join the brown dots to see what it looks like.

- Can you see what the house is called?

- **The house has a terrace overlooking the bay.**
  Find it by joining the green dots.

- **What can you see if you join the yellow dots?**

On the beach

- Mouse has been busy. Join the yellow dots to see what he has been doing.

- Join the red and blue dots to see what he used.

- Cat and mouse have had a picnic. Join the green dots to find their picnic hamper.

- Join the orange dots to find someone who would like to help finish the picnic.

1 2 3 4 5 6 7 8 9 10 11 12 13 14 15 16 17 18 19 20 21 22 23 24

In the water

- What is cat doing? Join the yellow dots to find out.

- Join the green dots to find out what the hedgehogs are doing.

- Who is splashing? Join the blue dots to see.

1 2 3 4 5 6 7 8 9 10 11 12 13 14 15 16 17 18 19 20 21 22 23

● Join the red dots to see what is lying on the beach.

● Who has fallen out of his boat?

A rock pool

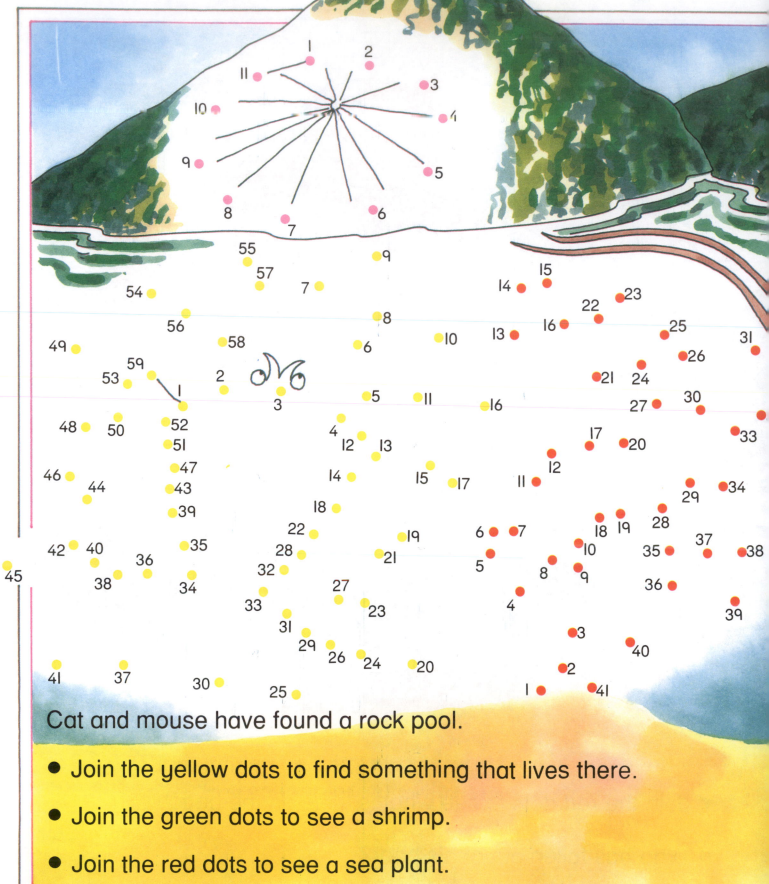

Cat and mouse have found a rock pool.

- Join the yellow dots to find something that lives there.

- Join the green dots to see a shrimp.

- Join the red dots to see a sea plant.

- If you join the blue dots you will see an animal that looks like a plant. It is called a sea anenome.

- Limpets stick very tightly to rocks. You can see one by joining the pink dots.

Watersports

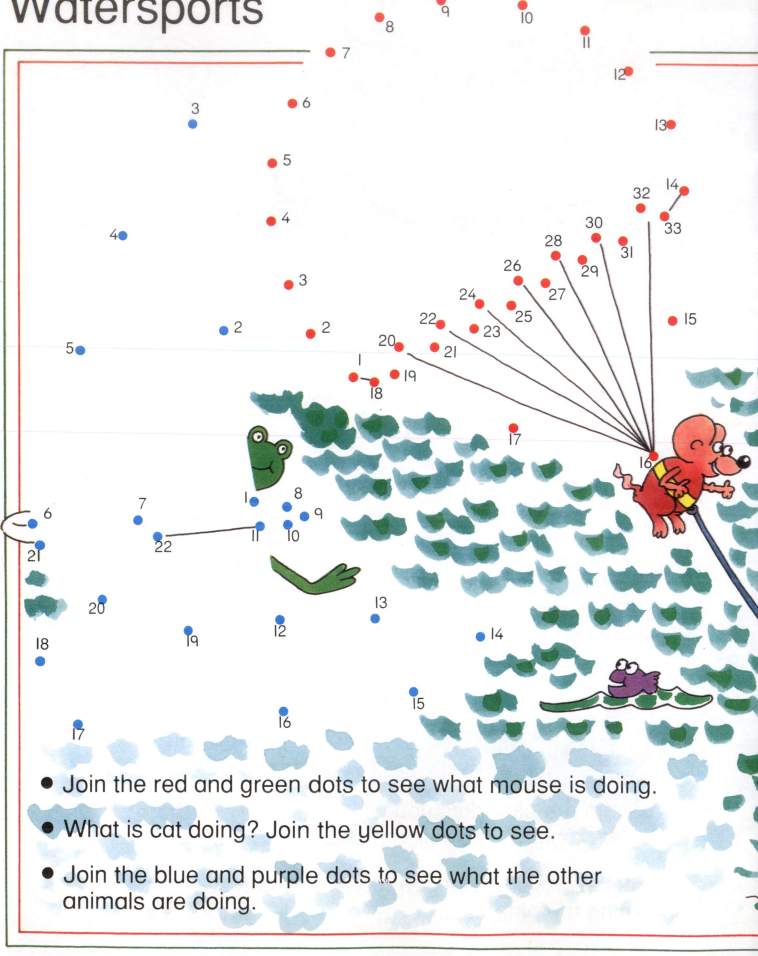

- Join the red and green dots to see what mouse is doing.

- What is cat doing? Join the yellow dots to see.

- Join the blue and purple dots to see what the other animals are doing.

1 2 3 4 5 6 7 8 9 10 11 12 13 14 15 16 17 18 19 20 21 22 23 24 25

The beach café

- Join the green and red dots to see the beach café.

- Who is pouring out drinks? Join the brown dots to see.

- Join the yellow dots to see what mouse has ordered.

1 2 3 4 5 6 7 8 9 10 11 12 13 14 15 16 17 18 19 20 21 22 23 24 25

- Join the blue dots to shade cat and mouse from the sun.

- Finish drawing their table by joining the orange dots.

- Mouse has lost his sunglasses. Can you find them?

26 27 28 29 30 31 32 33 34 35 36 37 38 39 40 41 42 43 44 45 46 47 48 49 50

The port

Join the blue and red dots to see frog's fishing boat and the hoists which he uses to unload his catch.

- Join the pink dots to find something which floats on air.

- What can you see if you join the yellow dots?

Underwater

Cat and mouse are scuba diving.

● Join the yellow dots to find out what cat is looking at.

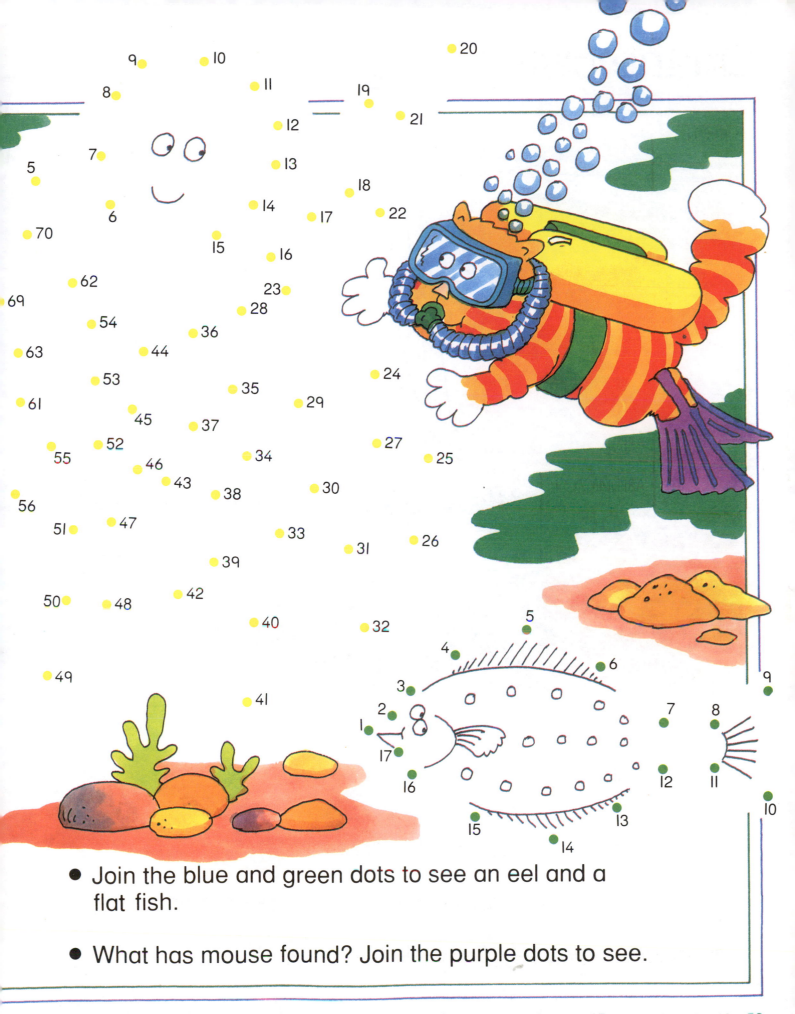

- Join the blue and green dots to see an eel and a flat fish.

- What has mouse found? Join the purple dots to see.

On the cliffs

Cat and mouse are going for a cliff walk.

● Join the blue dots to see who mouse is photographing.

● What can you see if you join the yellow dots?

1 2 3 4 5 6 7 8 9 10 11 12 13 14 15 16 17 18 19 20 21 22 23 24 25

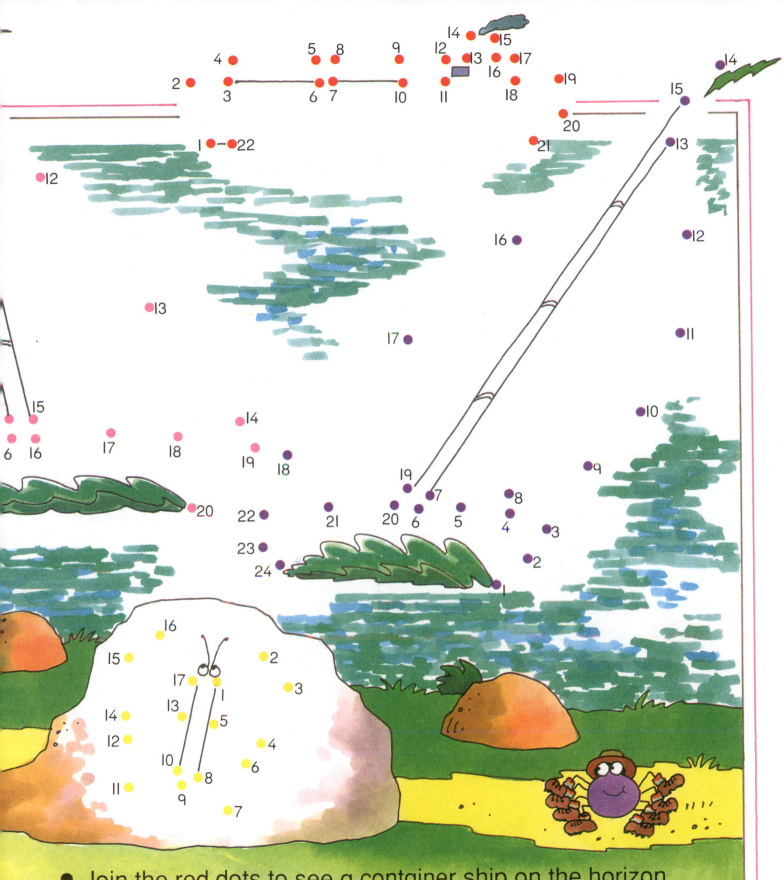

- Join the red dots to see a container ship on the horizon.

- If you join the green, pink and purple dots you will see some yachts racing. Which one is winning?

Buying souvenirs

Cat and mouse are looking for presents to take home.

● What can you see if you join the dots?

1 2 3 4 5 6 7 8 9 10 11 12 13 14 15 16 17 18 19 20 21 22 23 24 25

The Shell Shack

- Join the green and orange dots to see some gifts that are decorated with shells.

- Join the pink and yellow dots to finish the Shell Shack.

Home again

Cat and mouse are unpacking.

- Join the blue and yellow dots to see their suitcases.

- Join the green dots to see what cat bought himself at the Beach Bazaar.

- What did mouse buy at the Shell Shack? Join the red dots.